Journaling by the Moon

Written by Kim Galliher
Designed by Anissa Cosby

Get in touch

hello@journalingbythemoon.com

Created by: Kim Galliher
Designed by: Anissa Cosby
Edited by: Jessica K. Olsen

Graphic & Image Credits:

Vintage Moon Signs: Chikovnaya
https://stock.adobe.com/contributor/204622508/chikovnaya

Moon Calendar 2020: Paw
https://stock.adobe.com/contributor/203052872/paw

Moon Phases Icon: Maddyz
https://stock.adobe.com/contributor/205793653/maddyz

Stay Wild Moon Child: Mila Okie
https://stock.adobe.com/contributor/205487294/mila-okie

This Journal Belongs to:

_____

_____

_____

_____

_____

To my sister, Larkin, who celebrates my wins maybe more than I do. To my daughter, Skyler, who is always so proud and happy for me. For my son Hunter, daughter Mahayla, and husband Jeffrey, for their undying love and support. And for my mom, Linda, who supports me no matter what I happen to be doing. And for Anissa, for taking an idea and some words and turning it into a beautiful book.

-Kim

To my husband, Sharfiq, who has always supported my dreams from day one. To my kids, Isaiah, Ariel, and Abin, for always lighting up my life. For my sister, Maryann, and her undying support and love. For my mother, Audrey, for showing me what it means to be a magickal woman. And for Kim, who's words always teach me how to connect to my Divine and for writing this amazing book.

-Anissa

Foreword

Kim and I have never met face-to-face, yet she is someone I refer to as a kindred spirit. She has an innate ability to put you at ease through her genuine compassion and nurturing nature whether it's through her written or spoken words, which still come with a slight Texas drawl. The foundation for what would become "Journaling By The Moon" unwittingly began as a child for her within the "woo-woo" world as she refers to it. It has come to fruition after the culmination of Kim's lifelong experiences through daily meditation and learning, both informal and formal. She heard the calling to create a beautiful gift straight from her heart and soul in the form of this book. Through concise instructions and guidance that all women can take part in with ease, Kim shares her practices for harnessing the lunar energy throughout the different phases of the Moon for all of 2020!

Anissa is another soul sister that I nearly had the pleasure of meeting in person this year. It is through her own endeavors within the spiritual realm and talent as a graphic designer that she is able to translate Kim's beautiful voice into a visual masterpiece. As if that were not enough, Anissa created insightful and unique tarot spreads that complement the journey through each moon phase. These easy to follow, but reflective layouts appeal to both novice and experienced tarot users. They illustrate her passion for and understanding of the influences the Moon has on every woman!

-Jessica K. Olsen, Editor

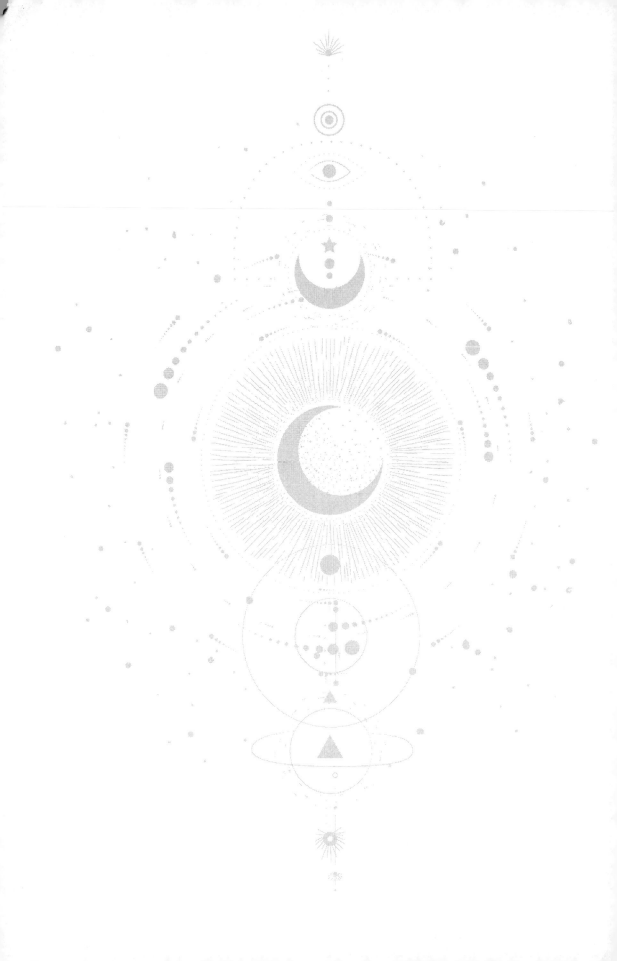

Table of Contents

2020 Moon Phase Calendar

Follow this quick Moon Phase Calendar to quickly see the phases in advance!

Please keep in mind that this journal starts with the New Moon on December 26th, 2019.

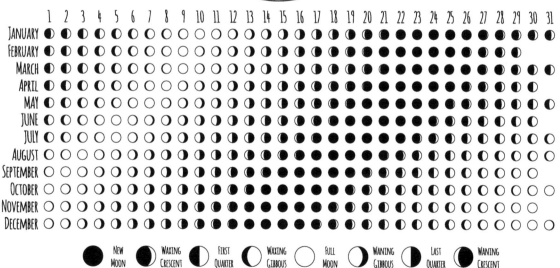

The Moon

She is as beautiful as she is mysterious. Her power is undeniable, as even the tides are willing to do her bidding. She is the symbol of the Divine Feminine. In many Wiccan practices, and for many pagans and witches, the Triple Moon Goddess is honored. Recognizing the cycles of the moon as the same cycles of women themselves.

Wise women (and even farmers) have long since known that each cycle of the moon brings a different kind of power, a different energy and have used that to their advantage in their healing and magick. And magick is just manifestation with empowered props after all. (wink, wink)

There is a resurgence of feminine power and with that comes a reconnection to the Divine Feminine and a reconnection to our innate spiritual selves, who we were before society told us to be something different.

Connecting with the moon is a connection with our deeper selves. A mixture of our Higher Selves and our Primal Selves at the same time. The wild natural side of things before rules stripped away our own power, our confidence, and trapped the Divine Feminine that resided inside us. Within these pages there are healing exercises to reclaim who you are meant to be. Let me rephrase that, who you truly ARE underneath all the layers of otherness.

So I welcome you, sister, to take part, to unfold, and become yourself.

ENJOY COLORING THE FOLLOWING PAGE!

Wheel of the Year Spread

This tarot spread is very helpful for mapping out your 2020 year and outlook. The Wheel of the Year Spread is a very popular spread that can assist you with your goals! You will use two cards per month, the card on the left represents the external factors to focus on, while the card on the right represents the internal factors to acknowledge. Be sure to write down notes on each of the cards, and reflect on them throughout the year!

JANUARY

Internal Card:	External Card:

FEBRUARY

Internal Card:	External Card:

MARCH

Internal Card:

External Card:

APRIL

Internal Card:

External Card:

MAY

Internal Card:	External Card:

JUNE

Internal Card:	External Card:

JULY

Internal Card: **External Card:**

AUGUST

Internal Card: **External Card:**

SEPTEMBER

Internal Card:	External Card:

OCTOBER

Internal Card:	External Card:

NOVEMBER

Internal Card:	External Card:

DECEMBER

Internal Card:	External Card:

New Moon

December 26th, 6:15pm PST | 9:15pm EST

It is perfect timing that the New Moon falls on December 26th, allowing us to say goodbye to 2019, and welcome in the brand new 2020. It truly is a time for new beginnings and big magick. So use your energy wisely, my friend. Tune in deeply, listen to your soul and hear what it is asking of you for this is the moment of moments. Your opportunity to set your intention, not just for January, but all of 2020.

So make a cup a tea or pour a glass of wine, and grab your journal (come on girl I know you have a new one picked out) and find a cozy corner to get real in.

- I want you to get still, close your eyes, and tune in to your heart's desires.
- If this was the year that ANYTHING was possible, you could have, do or go anywhere, what would that look like to you?
- Close your eyes and see, feel and know what that is.
- When you feel deeply connected to it, and can almost taste how wonderfully sweet it is, write it all down in your journal.

Once that is done, hold your non-dominant hand palm up towards the heavens and with your dominant hand on your open journal entry, call down the moon:

"Goddess energy, Divine Feminine that moves the tides and cools the earth beneath our feet, I call on you. I ask that you lend your power to my desires. As your light grows, my intention becomes manifest. And so it is."

Full Moon

January 10th, 11:23am PST | 2:23pm EST

The January full moon is known as the Wolf Moon in many parts. This is when the villagers would hear the wolves loudly howling because they had run out of food in the forest and had moved closer to town to feed. They were hungry and desperately seeking sustenance to carry them through to the spring.

We all go through stages of hunger. When we desire something so desperately we can almost taste it, but we become blinded by our hunger we don't see what is before our eyes. When manifesting it is difficult sometimes to let go and trust because we are so hungry for the results. We want it to just hurry up and happen already. But there is peace in letting go. And sometimes when you let go and stop trying to force the issue the miracle happens. Just like when you finally decide to get up and use the restroom at a restaurant and you return just as the waiter sets down the last plate. Just. Let. Go.

So again, find your quiet corner and grab your journal.
- I want you to think about in what small or large way have you been holding onto your desire instead of simply letting go?
- Are there patterns you create for yourself?
- Close your eyes and tune into this energy. See it, feel it or know it.
- However the information flows to you, just surrender and allow it to come.
- When you have fully connected, write it all down.

Once you have it all written down, place your dominant hand on your heart and your non-dominant hand palm up to the heavens and invoke the moon.

"Goddess, Divine Mother energy who balances out all that is masculine in this world. I ask that you help me release that which does not serve me. Allow me to simply let go, allow me to get into the Universal flow and simply be. Allow me to perfectly align with you and God/Universe/Source (pick what works for you). And so, it is."

New Moon

January 24th, 1:44pm PST | 4:44pm EST

With the New Moon in Aquarius, expect your emotions to be high this cycle. And that's ok. While Aquarius is the Water Bearer, she is a fixed Air sign. You can make an active choice to allow those emotions to drift away on the ethers. It may take conscious effort on your part, but you are in control of your story. You write the script. If things get too heavy where that decision becomes more difficult, pull out your handy-dandy journal and write it out. Look deep into those negative vibratory emotions such as anger, jealousy, fear and loathing. Feel and feels and then look to see WHY you are feeling them and deal with the why then move on to something better. However, do not let it fester by creating stories beyond the truth of the situation, making it worse and bringing you further down into the depths of negativity.

On this New Moon:
- Grab your journal and a pen.
- Pour yourself something relaxing to sip on.
- Set your Sacred Space.
- Light a candle (we have wonderful crystal Sacred Space candles in the shop).
- Burn some sage or incense, maybe diffuse some essential oil.

Answer these questions in your journal:
- What emotions am I feeling right now?
- How do I want to feel over the next cycle?
- What steps can I take to reconnect to those feelings when things go astray?

Affirmation: It is OK to feel my emotions.

One beneficial way to reconnect to our center is by grounding. Visit the link below to download a great grounding meditation:

https://www.spirituallifepathinstitute.com/digital-products/ground-surround-and-protect-meditation

You can also find wonderful crystal Sacred Space candles by visiting the link below:

https://www.spirituallifepathinstitute.com/shop/magic-fairy-sacred-space-candle

February 8, 11:34pm PST | February 9, 2:34am EST

February's Full Moon is named the Snow Moon because February historically brings much more snowfall than any other month. The Cherokee call it Bone Moon. They call it this because in times of the hunt, food supplies would run thin towards the end of winter. They would be down to the bare bones, making bone marrow soup or gnawing on bones for what remained. Thank goodness for easier times, right?

But winter brings about it this sense of emotional hardship even today, especially in parts of the country that experience more dark and dreary days than sunshine. So many people struggle with SAD and are craving for winter to end come February. They are desperate for warmer weather and sunshine.

Are you feeling desperate? Desperate for sunshine? Desperate for warmer weather? Leaves and flowers to make their appearance once again? Waiting for Mother Nature to manifest something other than cold and snow? Are you ready to trade your winter coat for flip-flops?

So on this Full Snow Moon
- Grab your journal and pen.
- Pour yourself something warm and inviting to drink.
- Find a quiet and cozy place to cuddle up.
- And set your Sacred Space.
- Light your candle, burn some incense, sage or diffuse your favorite essential oil. Just make sure it is safe for pets if you have them.

(Continued on the following page)

Full Moon (cont'd)

I want you to close your eyes and see, feel or know how you have not shown up for yourself over the last two weeks. The times you were passive instead of taking action towards what you are trying to manifest.. Were there opportunities where you could have played an active role in your own destiny? Or have you let the winter get the best of you and simply laid dormant, like the flowers and trees, waiting for a better day? You will close your eyes and see this about yourself. And when you connect and acknowledge your behavior and how it does not serve you, forgive yourself. And just let it all go. We are only human and now that you are conscious of the behavior, you can choose to make changes.

Write in your journal the behaviors that are no longer serving you on your path to success-whatever success looks like to YOU. Write whatever behaviors down you want to forgive and release into the ethers to be transmuted into love, that are keeping you from manifesting your desires.

When they are written down and you feel your list is complete, put your non-dominant hand palm up to the heavens and your dominant hand palm down on your list and say,

"I call upon the moon in all her glory, and the energy of the Divine Feminine, to transmute the energy of this list of things that no longer serve me into pure love. Send pure love back out into the Universe, making it a better place for every living being upon it. I am eternally grateful and blessed."

*NOTE-This is not a time to beat up on yourself. This must all be done with love. Becoming conscious is to become accepting of where you are right here and now. That is all we can do. We are simply acknowledging. Never judging. We are imperfect humans here to learn and we learn by doing and doing means making "mistakes" and trying again. We don't beat up on a baby when they get brave enough to take their first steps and constantly fall until they find their balance to stay upright on two feet. It should be no different as we learn as adults.

New Moon

February 23, 7:33am PST | 10:33am EST

The New Moon in Pisces invites us to be creative this month. It also strongly encourages you to expand your spiritual awareness. If you start to feel that ol' ascension flu, don't shy away from it, but accept it with grace. Pisces will be kind to you should you accept the challenge this month. So when working your manifestation magick this month, keep in mind that the spiritual and creative aspects are already strongly in your favor. Why not utilize the Universe's forward motion to propel you towards your goals in this area?

If you have an orange calcite, orange carnelian or tiger's eye stone grab those.
- Get your journal and a pen.
- Set your Sacred Space by lighting a candle. We have fabulous crystal New Moon Intention candles you can find HERE.
- Burn your favorite incense, sage, palo santo or diffuse some essential oil.
- Then ground yourself.

With the orange stone in your non-dominant hand, you will close your eyes for a moment and do this exercise. If you do not have an orange stone, place your hands above your Sacral Chakra. It is located about two inches below your belly button. You are going to connect with your Higher Self and your Sacral Chakra to see, feel or know what it feels like to give birth to the idea of what you want to create. Maybe it is something you've been wanting to create, but have put it on the back burner. Maybe it is something that has been just out of reach. Release and allow your Higher Self to come through and relay the information. If you are struggling to release control, picture yourself floating along on a raft, on a pond or river under a starry sky. You are looking at all the stars in the sky trying to make out constellations and wondering what they are and what they mean. And after floating along gently on the water and gazing up at the sky for a bit, you see written in the stars what it is you are meant to do.

Once you feel well connected to the concept of what you want to create, whether it's a picture, story, class, piece of pottery, business partnership, recipe, or anything else, open your eyes and write it down.

Full Moon

March 9, 10:48am PST | 1:48pm EST

March is commonly known as the Full Worm Moon. It's called this because in March the frost begins to fade, the ground softens and the earthworms return from their deep slumber and with it the return of the robins. Mother Nature is waking up and earth is once again becoming alive with activity.

What about you? Are you feeling more alive? Is there a spring in your step that wasn't there before? Does the sound of the birds singing in the morning put a smile on your face? Are you buzzing with anticipation about what is coming?

The full moon is also about the celebration of just being alive and feeling hopeful about what the future may bring.

- So grab your favorite beverage and have your favorite high vibe dancing playlist ready to go.
- Put that music on and grab your pen. This journal entry is just a list.
- List every good thing you have to be grateful for.
- What do you have to celebrate?
- Maybe life sucks right now and you have to break it down to the simple things-celebrating your ability to breathe, or your ability to see the world through your beautiful eyes.
- Maybe you are celebrating that someone was kind to you today, holding the door open for you instead of letting it fall shut as you stepped up to it.
- Whether big or small, there is always something to celebrate. Write it down!

Did your coffee this morning taste extra good because someone else made it for you? Celebrate! Did you use up the last of the toilet paper but had another roll on standby? Celebrate. Is the moon so incredibly gorgeous it takes your breath away? Celebrate! Look for all the reasons life is wonderful for you. Look for all the reasons YOU make life wonderful for others. Don't be afraid of celebrating your own damn self! You deserve it! And when you have written every little thing you can think of, dance like no one is watching. Better yet, take your music outside and dance under the light of the moon. Let it fill you with wild abandon and set you free. You are unfolding and becoming whatever you desire this season, so celebrate that too.

New Moon

March 24, 2:29am PST | 5:29am EST

The New Moon in Aries brings us a fiery new beginning, not just for this moon cycle, but for the astrological year as well since Aries is the first sign of the astrological calendar. With the New Moon in Aries, you can expect strong emotions to be present this month as Aries is full of them all and can flip from one emotion to the next in a second. Stay focused and use her fiery passion to take direct action and leave no prisoners in your wake.

Since Aries brings us this new beginning several months after our calendar new year, it is a great time to reassess. Take an introspective look and see where you would like to make a fresh start. During every new moon we have these fabulous mini-cycles to do this in.

So let's create your Sacred Space and get to journaling.
- Find a cozy spot.
- Grab something soothing to drink.
- Grab your journal and a pen.
- Smudge the space, light incense or diffuse your favorite essential oil.
- Ground yourself.

Consider now if you will about what your intentions were for the new year. What has been working for you, where might you be struggling, what needs to be sent on its way with love?

Let's look more closely at the places where you might be struggling. Can you see where improvements can be made? Are there realistic, actionable steps that you can take to make your dreams happen?

There is an old joke about how do you eat an elephant? One bite at a time. Is the picture simply too big to take in? When manifesting if we cannot get our minds behind the end result our mind cannot make our thoughts and energy believe it to be true. Sometimes it really does need to start with something very small and realistic. If the end result is too big to fathom, start with the first step. Manifest that. Then work on step two. Then three. Big pictures aren't created with a single stroke of a brush but by many, many strokes and sometimes various brushes and techniques. Don't be afraid to use ALL your brushes to create your work of art.

Full Moon

April 7, 7:35pm PST | 10:35pm EST

April is commonly known as the Pink Full Moon due to the pink phlox covering the ground at this time of year. Phlox is a ground covering that sprouts tiny, beautiful pink flowers. It's sometimes called pink moss. The pink phlox covers hillsides and the sides of roads and is stunning to look at, but you have to be careful because snakes and lots of other little critters feast on and take shelter in the low-lying flowers of the phlox. Sometimes we get so caught up and distracted by "shiny things" in life that we fail to pay attention to the danger signs around us. This could be signs from the Universe telling us to move in a different direction to our own gut instinct telling us not to do "that thing". Whatever it may be sometimes we don't tune in until after it is too late and we are left picking up the pieces.

Tonight that changes.

- Find a quiet place to lay down where you won't be disturbed.
- Ask your body to show you a "NO" answer.
- Once you feel it, ask your body to show you a "YES" answer.
- You are going to use your body similar to a pendulum. This is how you grow to trust and use your intuition on a regular basis.
- Once you have established yes and no, ask yourself an obvious YES question.
- Then ask yourself an obvious NO question.
- Test out the process with questions you know the answer to for a few rounds building up your confidence and then move on to questions you would like to know the answer to.

What do you need insight into? What area of your life has fear been holding you back in? Tap into that. See if your fear is legitimate, or if it is ego-based. Try it out and then write it out in your journal.

New Moon

April 22, 7:27pm PST | 10:27 EST

Things are about to get hot up in here! New Mc
about the physical, but mix that with the upcom
some very highly erotic energy going around. Roost...
deer are going to rut. EVERYONE is going to be feeling it.

Grab your journal and pen.
- Find your comfy spot or go to your designated space.
- Bring along a soothing beverage.
- Smudge the area, light some incense or diffuse essential oil.
- Cast your circle.
- Ground yourself.

Get very still and close your eyes.
- Tune in to your body.
- See what feels uncomfortable to you.
- Pay attention to that and take note.
- Now roll your head in one direction.
- Feel the stretch. Was it good? Roll it back the other direction.

Stretch your body in other ways. What other ways can you make yourself feel good tonight? Massage your shoulders? Feet? Do you have a spa you can slide into? A nice hot bath? Are there other things that you know that come to mind? Yes. I mean sex. With someone or by yourself. Or dance. Do yoga. Go for a run. Just get in touch with your body, make it work for you and celebrate that. Write it down how it made you feel. How joyous it is to be blessed with a fine working machine to house your soul.

Full Moon

May 7, 3:45am PST | 6:45am EST

May is known as the Full Flower Moon or the Full Corn Planting Moon. April showers bring May flowers after all. There are blooms everywhere this month. tThe moon shines her light bright down upon their sleeping heads, filling them full of sweet dreams so they can spend their days being a beautiful blessing for all the world to see and enjoy.

That's how Mother Nature shows up for us, let's dive into how you show up for the world.

- Grab your journal and a pen.
- Get into your sacred space.
- Smudge the area, light incense or diffuse your favorite essential oil.
- Cast your circle.
- Ground yourself.

Take a deep breath in and slowly let it out. You work hard every day being a light to others in some way. You may not realize it. And you probably don't get near the credit you deserve, but I guarantee you that someone's world is better off because of the sheer fact that you are in it. I want you to think about your day, or even go back a week, or the past month, and think about how you are showing up for yourself, for others, for your pets, for the planet. I want you to write it all down. You don't have to elaborate if you don't want to. You can do it in a list format or make it as detailed as you desire. But truly acknowledge the contribution you make in this world.

When you feel your list is complete, place your non-dominant hand on the paper and your dominant hand on your heart chakra and say

"I am a beautiful piece of this Universal puzzle. My contributions create an important thread that helps hold it all together."

New Moon

May 22, 10:39am PST | 1:39pm EST

This New Moon is in Gemini, which is ruled by Mercury. Mercury rules all forms of communication, so now is a good time to strike up conversations you've been putting off-waiting for that perfect moment. It's the perfect time to get your marketing in place for entrepreneurs by refining your message and putting it out into the world for the best possible reception. You want to get mushy and talk about your feelings with the guy you just started dating last month because you think he might be "the one"? Well, the stars are on your side even if it IS a little early in the game.

By now you know the drill.
- Grab your journal and a pen.
- Pour yourself something soothing to drink.
- Get into your safe zone.
- Smudge, light incense or diffuse oils.
- Cast your circle.
- Ground yourself.
- Take a nice, deep breath in and slowly let it out.

Close your eyes and think of a truth you've been dying to speak. but afraid it would ruffle someone's feathers, hurt their feelings, etc. Say it out loud. If you can't say it out loud, whisper it or write it down, but it's best if you speak the words and then write them down as well.

Once you've set those words free, dig deep for another truth. And then another. I want you to strive for at least 5 truths. Be honest. It's ok. We are talking about opening your throat chakra.

Opening your throat chakra and speaking your truth never has to be hurtful to another person. You can be honest and kind at the same time. Being unkind, or "brutally honest" is not the same thing as being truthful. That is just being an asshole. If being "brutally honest", is your go-to, then practice this exercise in reverse by speaking your truth with kindness.

Full Moon

June 5, 12:12pm PST | 3:12pm EST

This Full Moon is considered the Strawberry Moon. June is the month for gathering the sweet, luscious strawberries off the vine. Just ripe for the picking as they say.

Many of you won't get this reference, but some will understand what it's like roaming the country roads, or maybe even your own garden and checking the vine for berries. Are they ripe yet? The anticipation building...and being filled with disappointment when they are still yellow. Or worse yet, when the birds beat you to the few ripe ones, LOL. But on a perfect dayday with the sun shining overhead and maybe a few puffy white clouds in the sky, you set out just knowing that this is the day you will get your bucket of berries. And, there will be pie or cobbler and a happy belly at the end of the day. When you get to the vine, lo and behold, the perfect and mos beautiful berries stare back at you just waiting to be picked.

Get your journal and a pen.
- Pour yourself a glass of wine, maybe a cup of tea or a cool glass of water with some fruit.
- Smudge your space, light some incense, or diffuse an awesome essential oil.
- Cast your circle.
- Ground yourself.

Anticipation sometimes gets the best of us. And in manifesting, it can often get in our way. Our failure to release and fully give it to the Universe, can prevent it from happening. It's time to check yourself.

Take a deep breath in and slowly let it out. Gently, but truthfully, take a look at where you might be doggedly holding onto what you are trying to manifest. Are you worrying about it to death? Are you talking about it, thinking about it constantly? Or have you "given it to God" as the saying goes? I know how hard it is to not get overly excited. I know sometimes we just get manic about something we desire so badly. But, you have to take a step back and allow things to unfold. Loosen your grip.

(Continued on the following page)

Full Moon cont'd

June 5, 12:12pm PST | 3:12pm EST

I do a small Unbinding Spell when I need to release things in order to receive it.

Visit the link below to purchase my unbinding oil.
https://www.etsy.com/listing/705110312/magickal-oils-magical-oils-come-to-me

- You are going to want to tear a sheet out of your journal or use the sheet provided here and fill in the blanks.
- Take a moment to meditate on the things that are holding you back from receiving. What no longer serves you that you need to release.
- And then write those into the sheet provided or cut your piece of paper into strips about 2 inches wide.
- Write the following:

"I release (fill in the blank). It no longer has any power over me. It no longer possesses any control. I reclaim my power and I choose my path. And so it is. Thank you."

Once that is written, fold the paper AWAY from you. Anoint it in Unbinding oil if you have it. When anointing the paper, you will start from the side closest to you and move it away from you like you are throwing it away.

Next, light it on fire and let it burn in your burning bowl. While it burns, envision yourself being freed from the chains that bind you to these past thoughts, behaviors or habits. Personally, I envision Archangel Michael coming to cut away the chains that bind me to these negative thought patterns with his mighty sword. Do what works for you.

New Moon

June 20, 11:42pm PST | June 21, 2:42am EST

Cancer is the mother of the signs. She is nurturing and loving, but she is also moody, LOL! Expect to see your maternal instincts come out while working on pet projects. Are you going the extra mile to lend your support to something that doesn't have what it takes, but you know there's potential down deep in there somewhere?? Do you know if you love it enough there's the opportunity for success?

This month, you want to nurture the potential. TRY to look at it objectively and not through the rose-colored glasses of a mother in love.

Grab your journal and pen.
- Go to your sacred space.
- Bring along a soothing beverage.
- Smudge the area, light some incense or diffuse essential oil.
- Cast your circle.
- Ground yourself.

Call down the moon.

Feel the power coursing through you. Do this for several minutes letting the energy build.

This is the time of new opportunities. Unlimited potential. What are you offering to the world?

Ask the Divine Feminine, the ultimate mother, to show you your potential. Feel the energy and just listen.

When the visions, words or knowingness have come to you, give thanks and write it all down into your journal.

Spend the next two weeks taking actionable steps developing that potential.

Full Moon

July 4, 9:44pm PST | July 5, 12:44am EST

Also known as the Thunder Full Moon, this moon is when the deer antlers are in their glory stage. It is also the month of thunderstorms. Mother Nature showing her volatile side. Letting her voice be heard in the rolling thunder across the skies. In the Southwest, it's monsoon season. Storms roll across the valley in a fierce manner, flooding the roads and dried up waterways.

New Moon in Cancer brought us the nurturing side of Motherhood. During the full moon, we are feeling her stormy effects. She is lighting up our world in flashes and jolts of lightning, stating demands in loud claps of thunder. Motherhood is no joke at times. We can mean business when we need to, often after we've been ignored the first 7 times, but sometimes it's for effect to get our point across and show how strong and might we really are. You should never underestimate the will of a mother.

So grab a pen and your journal.
- Pour yourself something soothing to drink: a glass of wine, a cup of tea or cocoa, fruited water.
- Go to your sacred space.
- Smudge the area or light incense or diffuse essential oil.
- Cast your circle.
- Ground yourself.

Journal Questions
- Is there a place in your life you need to show some exterior strength?
- How can you represent that emotion in your life to that person or situation?
- Is this a person or situation where you have been lax about enforcing boundaries in the past?
- If so, why do you feel you allow your boundaries to be broken?
- How can you better enforce your boundaries in the future?

Affirmation:
Keeping strong boundaries is a form of self-care.

Plug this affirmation into your phone or write it on your bathroom mirror if you can't figure out the phone thing. Set timers in your phone 3-4 times throughout the day to say it 3 times with each alarm. Or, say it 10 times in the morning and 10 times at night if written on your mirror.

New Moon

July 20, 10:33am PST | 1:33pm EST

New Moon is still in Cancer for this go around. This moon is very much about forgiving and forgetting. Lately, there is a lot of talk about forgiving, but that doesn't mean you have to forget. It also certainly doesn't mean you ever have to welcome that person back into your life. But, as someone who has done MASSIVE amounts of healing work in my life, for MAJOR life-altering things, I can tell you that the nice thing about forgiveness IS the forgetting part. It allows you to free yourself from that never-ending story that plays itself on a loop in your head every single day of your existence, reminding you just how miserable you really are. But forgiveness, when it is true and deep, disconnects you from that and sets you free. I wish that for everyone.

Set your Sacred Space by grabbing a pen and journal but also grab something you can watch YouTube on.

- Get yourself something to drink.
- Go to your special place and relax.
- Light some incense, diffuse some oil or smudge.
- Cast your circle.
- Ground Yourself.

EFT is what helped me. If you can't book a personal session with me, a Certified EFT Practitioner and Teacher, then I hope you can find your way to our YouTube channel and watch the video there. Visit the link below to watch the EFT for Forgiveness video.

https://youtu.be/E5y5Difn9TU

Full Moon

August 3, 8:59am PST | 11:59am EST

August is the month when the Great Lakes were most notably full of sturgeon and became the name for the full moon in August. Native Americans were so grateful for the bounty they were blessed with, that they dedicated a moon to it. Can you imagine being so filled with awe that you dedicate a full month to it? TIme is something we feel we have so little of these days that we are selective about what we are willing to dedicate our time, attention, and effort to.

Moans. Whenever a new endeavor is suggested, we often mutter the words, "I don't have time". But, if it were really a priority, we would make the time. Aren't you worthy of being a priority and making time for?

So grab your pen and your journal. Pour yourself something refreshing to drink.
- Gather in your sacred space.
- Light incense, smudge or diffuse your favorite essential oil.
- Cast your circle.
- Ground Yourself.
- Meditate for 2-3 minutes.

Tune in to the concept of what you are most grateful for in your life. ABefore you state the obvious answer of "family", it would be great if you chose something else. I know you show up for them every day, but this is about showing up for yourself, too. Connect with something else you are grateful for.

Once you identify what you are grateful for and are emotionally tied to it, ask yourself: How can I be present for and dedicate myself to honor what I am most grateful for until the next full moon?

Journal your ideas, both big and small, and see what you can come up with. This gives you options for those super busy days. Try to come up with several ways you can pay homage to the things that matter most in your life as a way to say "thank you". Maybe it is meditating on it, lighting a candle on your altar and saying a prayer of gratitude, or some other awesome way that I can't even fathom while writing this! I invite you to share your ideas on our page as we're learning and growing on this journey together.

New Moon ◎

August 18, 7:42pm PST | 10:42 EST

New Moon in Leo will leave you wanting a little praise for your hard work. Ok, not a little praise but ALL the kudos and maybe a few extra. The thing is about the New Moon being in Leo is, that while we love and desire that appreciation so very much, we really don't want to be in the spotlight because that opens us up to criticism. And if there's one thing Leo doesn't like it is criticism. So how do you go about getting the recognition you feel you deserve, but without getting picked over with a fine-toothed comb?

Well, you can validate yourself. Recognize your own worth, claim it, and wear it well. Or you can cozy up to others in the hope that they will sing your praises. If they find your shortcomings, realize we all have them and find ways to improve or work around them. In business, I have a lot of shortcomings and try to hire out for the things I am lousy at. I don't bother trying to master things I am not naturally skilled in, but instead focus my time and energy on things I know I can excel in. Pick your battles!

So let's gather your supplies.
* Grab a pen and your journal.
* Get something yummy to drink and maybe a piece of chocolate or a cookie.
* Find your comfy spot.
* Smudge, diffuse your favorite oil or burn some incense.
* Cast your circle.
* Ground yourself.

(Continued on the following page)

New Moon cont'd

August 18, 7:42pm PST | 10:42 EST

Meditate 2-3 minutes. Ask the Divine Feminine within you to open up and be honest during this exercise.

Where are you falling short right now? Don't judge just acknowledge. Become conscious. There is no room for judgment and belittlement. Write it down.
Are there areas you can delegate to someone else? Hire someone else to do?

If there is absolutely no way on earth to do either, is there some change you can make to improve your process?

Now set that thought aside.

Where in your life are you kicking ass? Don't be shy. I know there is some area of your life you are nailing it, so write it down. Tell yourself how awesome you are just like you were telling one of your children or a best friend. DO NOT HOLD BACK.

When you are done, put the palm of your non-dominant hand up towards the heavens and your dominant hand on your heart and call down the moon.

"I call on the moon in all its beautiful glory. Her power to turn the tides and so deeply affect our emotions. I ask that the Divine Feminine outside of me, to ignite the Divine Feminine inside me. Lending me the strength and courage to be my true self without apologies. To accept who I am with all my gifts as well as any shortcomings. To recognize that I am perfect even with all my imperfections. While I may strive to be better I know that I am always enough. And so it is. Thank you."

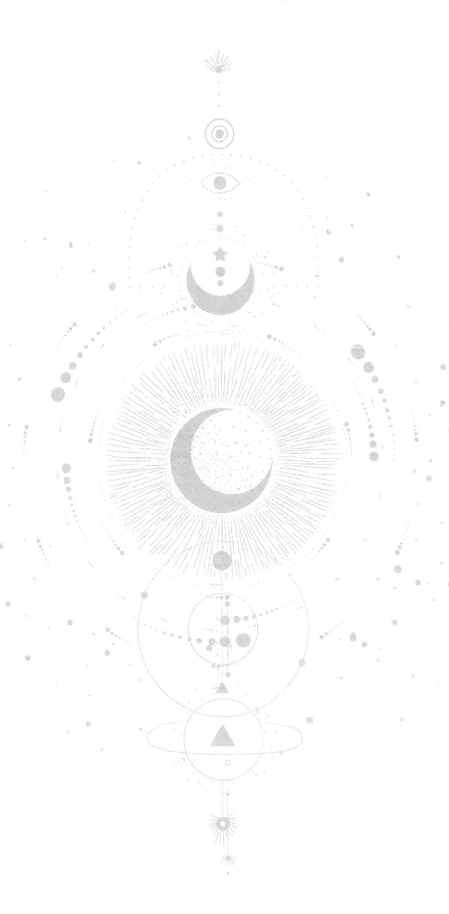

Full Moon

September 1, 10:23pm PST
September 2, 1:23am EST

The Harvest Full Moon represents the month for harvesting. Bringing in the goods for the fall and winter months to help fatten the stores for the colder months. Working the fields and reaping what you've sown.

The time every farmer has been waiting for. They've planted the seeds, fertilized, fought off pests, and hope and prayed the elements were kind to them. And NOW is the time to reap their sweet reward. And it's time for you to take note of all you've reaped as well.

Get your journal and a pen.
- Pour something wonderful to drink.
- Go to your comfy spot.
- Diffuse some essential oil, smudge or burn some incense.
- Cast your circle.
- Ground yourself.
- Meditate 2-3 minutes.

You are just going to tune in and note what has come to pass. All the good things that have come into existence. That's right, one big long gratitude Universal love fest.

I want you to use the format below. And if there is something in the works I want you to add it as if it was already yours as well.

Use the following statement:
'I am so incredibly excited now that I have _____ because now I can

_____. Thank you God/Universe/etc for making it so."

Write it out as many times as necessary. The more the better. Take a break if your hand gets tired. That just means you are very blessed.

Pre-Order the 2021 Moon Journal!

Now that you've learned to call down the moon, set a sacred space, and create a ritual it's time to move beyond. Way beyond.

Visualize, imagine, or pretend…
You are standing outside under the light of the moon. There are a few wispy clouds, but She is shining brightly. The air is crisp but pleasant. The spring equinox is right around the corner.

You can smell the power in the air, it smells of ozone. Your hair blows in the gentle wind leaving you feeling so empowered.

You decide now is the time to get to work. You cast your circle. Perhaps you have a wand or just use the power of your forefinger. Either way, the power is within you and it is dying to come out. And unleash it you will.

You tuck away your wand and stand in the center of your circle. You lift one hand to the heavens and the other down towards Mother Earth, throw your head back to gaze upon the glorious moon and call her down to reside within you. The Divine Feminine is one with you.

Now.

Now is the time to work your magick.

Join us for next year's journal. It's going to get a little wild.

What you will find…
- All new rituals for 13 moons, including outdoor rituals
- Moon Cycle Crystal Guide
- Rituals for the Solstices
- Rituals for the Equinoxes
- All new tarot spreads
- And more!

Pre-order yours today!

PRE-ORDER NOW!
AMAZON &
BARNES & NOBLE
$24.99

PRE-ORDER NOW!
www.journalingbythemoon.com

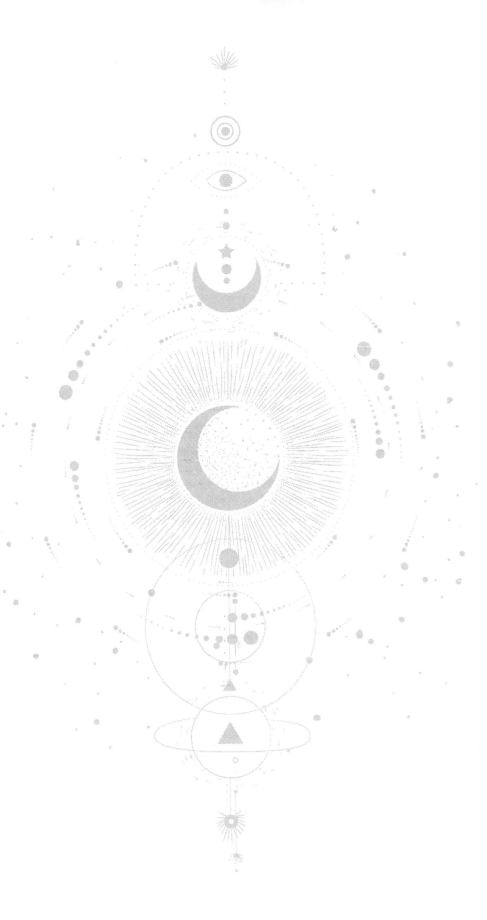

New Moon

September 17, 4:00pm PST | 7:00pm EST

New Moon in Virgo tells us to get our shit in order, LOL! All those disorganized nooks and crannies, that junk drawer you can barely open, the clothes you've been swearing you will fit into again since 2001--all of it. Virgo demands it must be dealt with. It's like nesting without the baby to show for it. Spring cleaning without the spring. Now is as good a time as any to utilize this powerful energy to get things in order.

Our minds might be feeling that extra bit of busyness too. Trying to organize our thoughts and ideas and turn them into something productive. Virgo loves a plan of action.

So let's utilize that energy and that of the new moon to create something powerful for ourselves.
- Grab a pen, your journal and something to drink.
- Go to your Sacred Space.
- Light your incense, smudge or diffuse essential oil.
- Cast your circle.
- Ground yourself.

Meditate 2-3 moments. Let your busy mind settle on the one idea you've been swirling around in your head over the last few days, weeks, maybe even months. Now is the time to address it and make it happen. Connect with that idea.

Journal questions:
- What is it about this situation that speaks to you?
- Would manifesting it improve your life? Would it make you happier?
- What 3 things can you DO to get the ball rolling starting tonight? Not in the morning. Not next week. But tonight after this exercise?
- Is there fear surrounding the idea of doing these things? Are you already trying to make excuses? What are they? Write them down.

(Continued on the following page)

New Moon cont'd

September 17, 4:00pm PST | 7:00pm EST

Now with your non-dominant hand palm up towards the sky and your dominant hand on your 3rd chakra (2 inches above your belly button) and call down the moon.

"Beautiful moon that watches over us as we sleep, wash down over me, come into me now. Divine Feminine and all the strength and beauty you represent, come into me now and connect with the Divine Feminine within me. Ignite the power within me. Help me find strength where I feel weakness. Help me see solutions where I see doubt. And so it is. Thank you."

With your dominant hand still on your solar plexus, close your eyes and see the solution to the issues you raised. See how you can make it all come together and work in your best interest.

Write the solutions down so they stay in your mind.

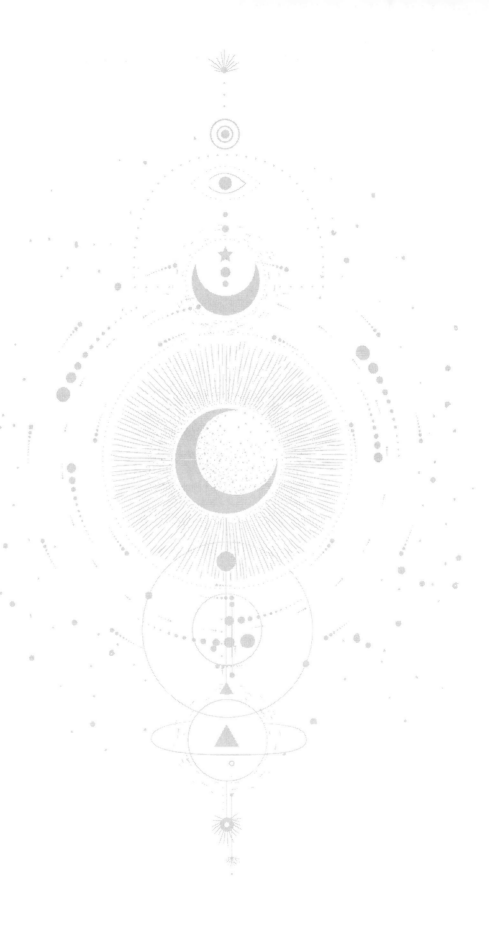

Full Moon

October 1, 2:06pm PST | 5:05pm EST

This is the Hunters Full Moon.. Tracking the deer, bison, elk whatever it was to sustain the tribe for the duration of the cold, dry months. With some luck and skill, there would be plenty to make it through a long, hard winter.

While we may no longer need to hunt, fish or even farm out of sheer necessity we do have skill sets that we need in order to survive. It's those that we need to focus on and be thankful for right now. It's those skills that are still putting food on the table, putting a roof over our heads, keeping our family warm and safe, clothed. You get my point.

Grab a pen and your journal.
- Pour yourself a glass of wine, cup of tea or maybe some fruited water. A piece of chocolate or cookie is also very grounding.
- Find your comfy spot.
- Burn some incense, diffuse your favorite oil or smudge.
- Cast your circle.
- Ground yourself.

Meditate 2-3 minutes.
Tune in to what skill sets you have that help you and your family survive. Even if you are a SAHM, you have very valuable skills that help make this happen. It isn't just about "earning a living". We are looking for skills beyond making money. DO NOT DISCOUNT YOURSELF. Everyone has skills. Don't start to fret if nothing comes immediately to mind, go back to your meditation and ask your Divine to show you.

Once you have your list of skills in mind, write them down and explain how valuable each one is to have. How your life, and the life of others-people or animals-if they are in the picture, depend on your great skill set. Tell the story. You play an important role in your life and the lives you touch. I want you to see it in just this one simple way. The sheer necessity of your existence. Write it all down.

Plug this affirmation into your phone or write it on your mirror. If setting timers in your phone, set 3-4 throughout the day and say it 3 times each alarm. If writing it on your mirror, you will say it 10 times each morning and night.

Affirmation:
My life has great meaning. My existence has such importance to so many in my life. I am grateful to be able to play such a big role.

New Moon

October 16, 12:32pm PST | 3:32pm EST

New Moon in Libra brings about a time of peace and harmony (or a need thereof). Striving for balance in your life is of the utmost importance. Getting in self-care before the hectic holidays is just what the Astrology Doctor ordered it seems. So get into the universal energy and just allow it to happen. It's ok to just be. You don't always have to be hustling and bustling.

Grab your journal and a pen.
- Make something yummy to drink, a glass of wine, cup of tea, how about a steaming cup of cocoa?
- Go to your peaceful place. (I call it my Zen Den)
- Burn some incense, smudge or diffuse your favorite essential oil blend.
- Cast your circle.
- Ground yourself.

I love this app so very, very much and I apologize if it is not on android but I really hope it is. It's called **Simply Being**. It's only $1.99. Go now and download it. Don't wait. Do it now.

This is going to be your best friend. If you struggle with meditation, this My Love will be a lifesaver. I tell my meditation students to download this app to help them learn how to sit in meditation. Guided meditation is different than sitting in meditation. It occupies different parts of the brain and while both are great ways to relax they have other different benefits.

Sitting in meditation not only calms the amygdala but it stimulates the prefrontal cortex where the sense of happiness lies. This is what our goal is-calm the reptilian brain and stimulate the higher mind.

The Simply Being app is a perfect combination between sitting in meditation and guided meditation. It helps train your brain to sit with your thoughts with just enough mental stimulation to not drive you absolutely batty and fidgeting off your cushion.

So download the app and get to meditating.

Blue Moon

October 31, 7:51am PST | 10:51am EST

Once in a blue moon...

Blue moons are the second full moon in a calendar month, and come about once every 33 months. While they're more common than the old saying sounds, they're still rare enough to make us stop and take pause.

Today is the day, and the moment is now that I want you to pause and take note of some very special things. That's what I want to focus on. What I've come to realize with so many women, including myself, is that knowing ourselves as ourselves can truly be a rare event.

Your preferences are often dictated by what your significant other or children like or dislike. We want to give ourselves so completely to those we love that we often lose sight of who we truly are. It's only after the divorce or the children have left the home that we are scrambling to figure out who we are again.

But what if you don't wait? What if you seize this moment? Take this somewhat are event that we ooh and ahh over and delve into yourself? It's a Blue Moon, after all, that's pure magick in and of itself.

So gather your supplies.
* Get your journal and pen.
* Pour yourself a nice glass of wine, cup of tea or maybe some cocoa.
* Diffuse some essential oils, burn incense or smudge your space.
* Settle into your Sacred Space.
* Cast your circle.
* Ground yourself.

(Continued on the following page)

Blue Moon cont'd

October 31, 7:51am PST | 10:51am EST

Close your eyes and think about who you were BK. Before kids or before your relationship. Maybe even before that job that runs your life.
SEE who you used to be before life colored your existence.
What foods did you like to eat?
What music did you like to listen to?
What clothes did you just HAVE to have? (It's ok to laugh at yourself at this one if you're going back decades.)
When you were wild and free what did your heart speak about what your soul loved to do? How did it sing out its existence into the Universe?

Now, I want you to think about the things you love now. You may have to start very small.

I don't want these to be things you like together with someone. If you are someone who always has a Facebook profile picture with someone instead of just your beautiful, shining self I want you to pay close attention to this exercise.

What do YOU love? Things that belong to YOUR heart? Write it all down.

When you have it written down go back and make dates with yourself to have more of these things in your life. Don't make them once in a blue moon occurrence.

All Hallows Eve!

All Hallow's Eve, now known as Halloween, began in the 8th century as the Christian response to Samhain. We couldn't let the Pagans have all the fun, now could we?

Samhain was known to be the day the veil was thin between the two worlds-the After World and this one. Pagans would build great bonfires, have celebratory feasts, try to converse with their loved ones on the Otherside and tell each other's fortunes. It was a wonderful day and evening of fun and festivities.

The Christian version was a bit more staunch and less celebratory but they would honor the saints and pray for souls who were caught in limbo or who had not yet reached Heaven.

The idea was to still have a holiday while covering the same premise to woo pagans into converting. I like wooing much more than I do burning them at the stake or such nonsense as that. Gentle persuasion is always best in my book.

Nowadays, we celebrate with spooky decorations, scary movies and LOTS of candy but the veil is still thin and those of the witchy persuasion still have their ways.

So what can you do to celebrate?

- Set a place of honor for your loved ones at the table. Leave a sweet treat on your altar for them or even better something specific that they liked on the physical plane. Place their picture on your altar and say a prayer in remembrance.
- Have a bonfire or cozy up to your fire pit and count your blessings.
- Do a reading for yourself or a friend in whatever type of divination you connect with.
- Light some incense, get quiet and try to connect with a loved one who has passed on. Do not discount smells you may get or memories you suddenly recall this is how spirit speaks to us.
- Cook up some yummy fall treats and share with family and friends. I love warm wassail. And vegan shepherd's pie with root vegetables. Cook things in the fall spirit.

Try any or all of these but most importantly have fun!

New Moon

November 14, 9:08pm PST | Nov. 15, 12:08am EST

Well, things are about to get a little in intense. Intense emotionally. Intense mentally and intense sexually. Scorpio is just intense energy. Nothing shallow about it, if anything it may be a little too deep for its own good.

Be mindful if you are wearing this energy like a heavy coat. Don't be afraid to get centered and slip right out of it or at least take a layer off so you aren't getting into that whole Emo effect. Trying it on for a day is one thing but trying to make the fashion trend come back is a definite no-no.

Set your sacred space by getting some tea, wine, fruited water or cocoa to drink.
- Grab a pen and grab your journal.
- Grab a piece of selenite or black tourmaline.
- Diffuse some essential oil or burn some sage or incense.
- Cast your circle.
- Ground yourself.

Journal Questions:
- What emotions are you most in touch with right now?
- What do you feel is most YOU? What feelings do you feel are coming from outside? NOT you?
- During this busy time of year when we seem to be surrounded by the company of others so often we need time to decompress. What are 5 ways you can think of to make time for yourself to just BE? Realistic things you can make time for and actually do?

Take a sheet of paper and cut it into strips or use the one provided and cut it. Write the following or fill in the blanks.

I am feeling _____ but this emotion is not my own. I am setting it free. This stone transmutes the energy of that emotion and sends it back into the Universe pure and wholesome.

While saying this statement, hold the stone and the paper between your two hands at heart center, as if in prayer. You may burn the paper afterward.

Full Moon

November 30, 1:32am PST | 4:32am EST

The Full Beaver Moon is the perfect time to set your beaver traps so that you might catch the beaver before the freeze. The goal being to gain their pelts to keep warm for the winter, insulating yourself from the harsh elements.

What do you do to protect yourself from outside influences? It is through our auras and our chakras that we take in energy around us-from other people, places, and things. This can be in a good way, but most often an overwhelming and negative way. It leaves us with emotions that aren't ours and anxiety we don't want to have. As someone whose strongest psychic ability is clairsentience I will tell you it truly helps.

Get your pen and journal.
- Pour yourself something nice to drink.
- Go to your comfy spot.
- Smudge, diffuse oils or light incense.
- Cast your circle.
- Ground yourself.

Now I want you to do this. Go to the link below and download the Ground, Surround and Protect meditation. Use code **PROTECT** to get it free.

https://www.spirituallifepathinstitute.com/digital-products/ground-surround-and-protect-meditation

Listen to it.

Journal how you feel afterward.

Use this meditation every day for at least the next 14 days.

New Moon

December 14, 8:18am PST | 11:18am EST

With New Moon in Sagittarius optimism is something that you should have in spades right now. The energy is just aligned for feeling positive and having faith that everything will go your way. So how do you get to go from FEELING that way to actually GOING that way? With a little manifesting magick.

Sarah Prout, a well-known Manifesting Queen has a 5x55 method that works like a charm.

For 5 CONSECUTIVE days you write a power statement 55 times. If you miss a day, you have to start over. You do it similarly to one we've already used here. Use descriptive words, state it as already having it, what you are using it for or why you are grateful and that you are grateful to your Divine.

Example: I am thrilled and overjoyed to have an extra $10,000 so I can get my daughter braces. Thank you God/dess/Universe/etc for your blessing.

Do this to manifest your desires.

When you are done. Take the sheets, fold them up and put them away where you will ALMOST forget about them and move on with your life.

Be sure to use a notebook or loose leaf paper when doing this exercise and then use the journal pages to journal your thoughts on the process.

Full Moon

December 29, 7:30pm PST | 10:30pm EST

The December Full Moon is known as the Cold Moon. It's when the cold comes creeping across the land, pushing out any last dregs of warmth. The fires are burning bright in the hearths and soups are being cooked in the kitchen. Soups were a great winter's meal because it used the meat and fall root vegetables in the cellars and made them stretch while filling the belly with something warm. (As I write this, corn chowder is on the menu for us tonight!)

The nights are long and the days short. There's a lot of time to be left with your own thoughts. It is these thoughts that we're after. It's time to get introspective. And then, we dance. There should always be dancing. But first we go within.

Grab your pen and your journal.
- Pour yourself something delicious to drink. Warm wassail sounds great!
- Go to your cozy spot.
- Smudge, light some incense or diffuse some essential oil.
- Cast a circle.
- Ground yourself.

This is the last full moon for the year and of this journal. The time to be both introspective and celebratory.

Journal questions:
Looking back over the past year-
- What were your big wins?
- Where did you fall short?
- In the areas where you fell short, do you need to regroup and find a better way to move forward next year? Or do they need to be released?
- What benchmarks do you want to set for yourself for 2021?

Break it down into smaller pieces and do JUST the first quarter of 2021.
- List 5 actionable steps you can take to get there.
- List 3 things you need to let go of in order to reach those goals with confidence.
- List 3 things you can do to show yourself great love when you need a pep talk.

Now put on some high vibe music and dance like no one is watching. Really shake your groove thing. We are letting it all go. Right. Now.

Good-bye resistance. Good-bye fear. Good-bye 2020.

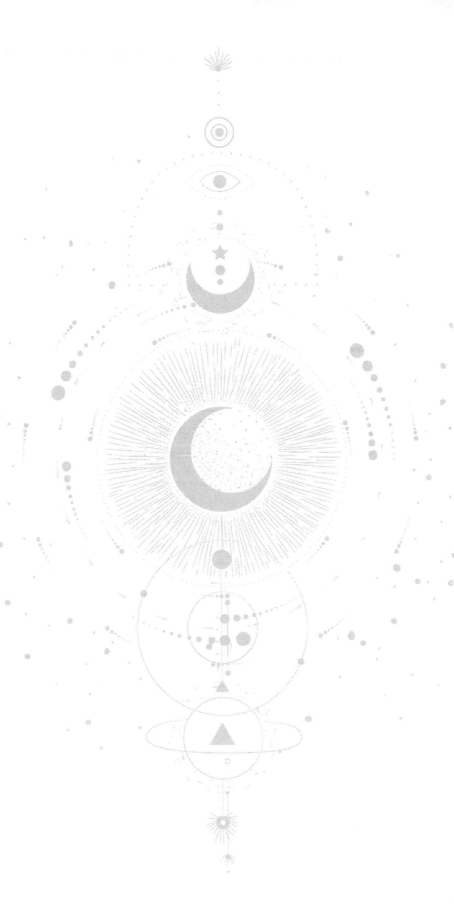

Tarot are the answers we seek...

They're already there, inside. Can't you feel it?

The following pages are filled with tarot spreads that can guide you throughout the year for a multitude of reasons. The tarot can be a powerful spiritual tool that aides and guides you to o the answers you seek. The purpose of the tarot is to give us confirmation of what is already known deep down inside. Spirit comes to use through the cards and enlightens us on our journey.

Tarot is helpful for a multitude of reasons including:
- Spiritual Advice from God/dess
- Clarity on Situations
- Shadow Work
- Spiritual Healing
- Clarity on Purpose
- And much more.

So dive in and let the tarot guide you to the answers you seek!

Here are some steps you should take before doing your reading:
1. Prior to performing your reading, make sure that you're in a quiet place and have cast a circle around your space. The purpose of this is to keep negative energy out and to keep it from swaying your reading. This also protects you and allows you to get real quiet with Spirit.
2. If you have sage, light some sage to clear the air and clear the cards.
3. Set the intention that you want to clear your spiritual blocks and that you'd like Spirit to assist you with clearing those blocks.
4. Shuffle the cards until you feel content and ready to stop.
5. Perform your reading!
6. After your reading, remember to thank Spirit (Goddess) for giving you Her wisdom.
7. Clear off any residual energy. I like to shake myself a bit and I have selenite to hold on to in order to ground my energy. You can also lightly meditate on the reading results as well. This is the time to also open your circle to release that energy as well.

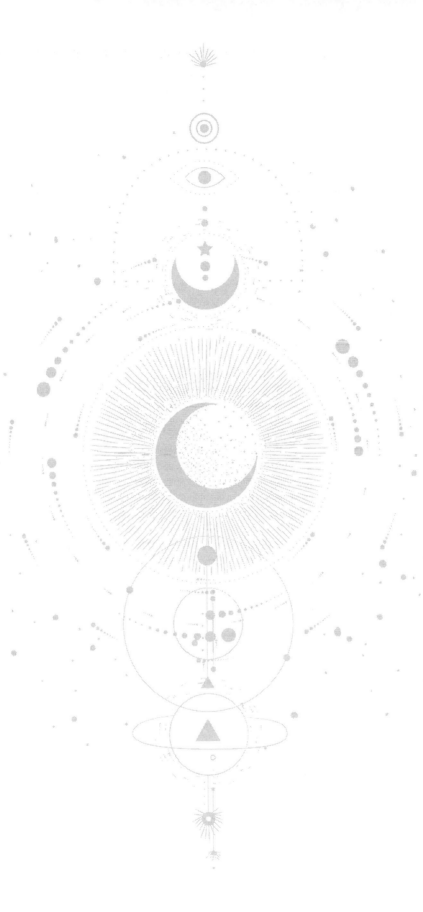

New Moon Spread

Use this Tarot Spread with Each New Moon

With each New Moon, setting intentions are helpful because the new moon reminds us to start fresh. This spread allows you to reflect at where you are, where you'd like to go and how to get there.

CARD 1: WHERE AM I AT NOW?
CARD 2: WHERE DO I WANT TO BE?
CARD 3: HABITS & STRENGTHS TO DEVELOP AND NURTURE
CARD 4: RELATIONSHIPS TO DEVELOP AND NURTURE
CARD 5: KNOWLEDGE AND SKILLS TO LEARN OR IMPROVE
CARD 6: WHERE TO FOCUS MY INTENTIONS

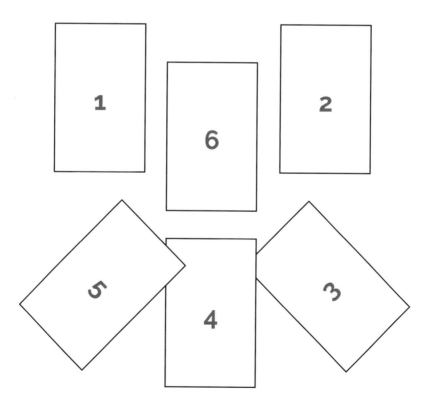

Full Moon Spread

Use this Tarot Spread with Each Full Moon

With each Full Moon, we take on things that need to be released. Releasing shouldn't be reserved as a one-time thing. The more we release, the more we make room for things that make us happy. Use this spread to guide you in your release.

CARD 1: WHERE AM I AT NOW?

CARD 2: THINGS FROM THE PAST I'M CLINGING TO

CARD 3: EXPECTATIONS FOR THE FUTURE I AM CLINGING TO

CARD 4: HABITS OR BEHAVIORS HOLDING ME BACK

CARD 5: RELATIONSHIP BOUNDARIES TO SET

CARD 6: WHAT NEEDS TO BE RELEASED

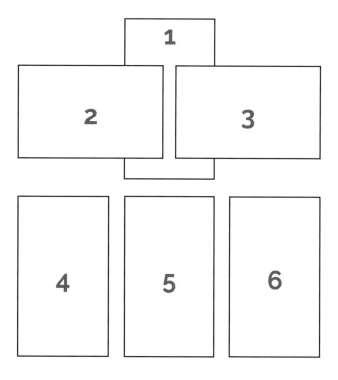

Crossing the Bridge Spread

On our journey in life, we often come to major moments in the "road" where we have to make a decision. We come across crossroads and bridges that lead us to places that we yet to know the outcome. When creating this spread, I was literally waiting at the proverbial bridge, wondering if I had the courage to take the first step into the unknown. What was on the other side? I had no clue, but I knew that if I didn't do something, that the bridge would disappear and I'd have to find another way around.

Are you at the bridge? Ready to cross over but feeling a sense of fear? Then this spread will help clear up the fog, so that with guidance from Spirit, you can have an idea of what you need to release so that you can cross over into your future.

CARD 1 - FEARS WHAT FEARS DO I HAVE?

CARD 2 - TIES WHAT/WHO IS HOLDING ME BACK?

CARD 3 - 1ST STEP WHAT IS MY FIRST STEP TO TAKE?

CARD 4 - HOW? HOW DO I TAKE THIS FIRST STEP?

CARD 5 - WELCOME! WHAT CAN I WELCOME INTO MY LIFE?

CARD 6 - OTHER SIDE WHAT CAN I EXPECT ON THE OTHER SIDE?

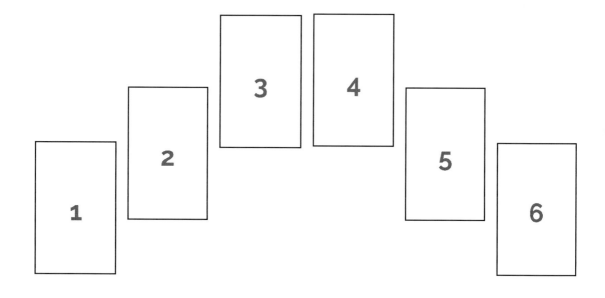

Uncovering Spiritual Blocks Spread

Often we have to take time to assess what our spiritual blocks are. This tarot spread will aid you in discovering what those are and how you can clear them.

CARD 1. SELF - THIS REPRESENTS THE READER.
CARD 2. SPIRIT - WHAT IS THE CURRENT STATE OF MY SPIRIT?
CARD 3. SHADOW - WHAT'S GOING ON IN THE SHADOW REALM?
CARD 4. BLOCKS - WHAT ARE MY CURRENT BLOCKS?
CARD 5. CLEANSING - WHAT CAN I GET RID OF THAT NO LONGER SERVES MY SPIRIT?
CARD 6. CARE - HOW CAN I CARE FOR MY SPIRIT MORE?

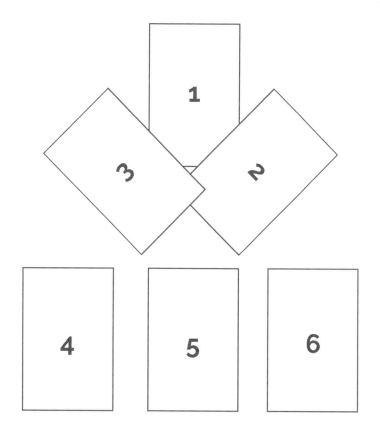

Mercury Retrograde Spread

Mercury Retrograde occurs 3-4 times a year and is completely unavoidable. Mercury Retrograde is a time where we need to focus on ourselves. With Mercury ruling over ALL communications, we might not make as clear decisions as we want to.

A Mercury Retrograde reading will help you decipher what you should focus on during the next 3.5 weeks so that you can come out on top after the fact.

While it's best to have your reading done at least 2 days prior to Mercury Retrograde, it's never too late to have it done. Even if you're already in the middle of the retrograde and need some guidance!

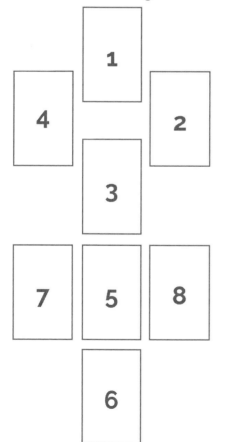

CARD 1: WHAT IS MY INTUITION TELLING ME?

CARD 2: WHAT SHOULD I IMPROVE ON DURING THE RETROGRADE?

CARD 3: WHAT INTENTIONS SHOULD I SET?

CARD 4. WHAT SHOULD I LET GO?

CARD 5. HOW CAN I OPEN UP TO RECEIVE?

CARD 6. HOW CAN I GIVE BACK?

CARD 7. HOW CAN I TAKE CARE OF MYSELF?

CARD 8. WHAT IS SPIRIT TELLING ME TO FOCUS ON?

2020 MERCURY RETROGRADE DATES

February 17 – March 10: in Pisces & Aquarius

June 18 – July 12: in Cancer

October 14 – November 3: in Scorpio & Libra

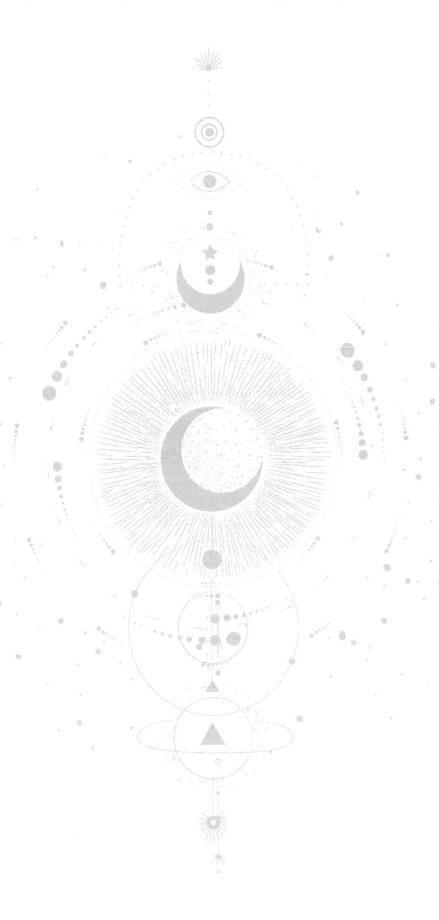

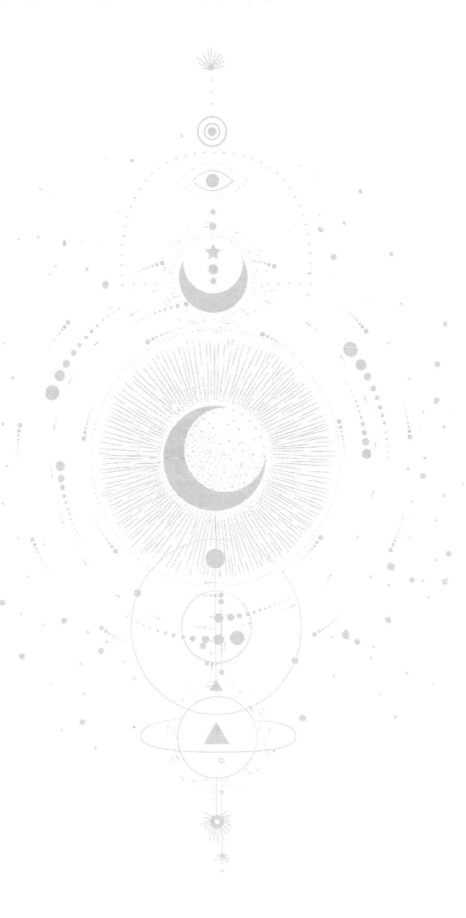

Final Thoughts

You made it through 13 glorious moons. An entire year of transitions and rituals. You've had plenty of introspection and celebration of self. You learned how to call down the moon and what that wonderful energy feels like. We hope that you learned to trust your intuition, feel more empowered in your rituals, and are now practicing grounding every day.

Grounding, surrounding, and protecting can help get you through so many rough times. And just pausing to ground can bring you back to the center of calm and focus when things get stressful.

Our wish for you is that you felt within you the rise of the Divine Feminine.

She is not simply outside of you. She is you. She is part of your Higher Self. When you are putting yourself together in the morning, visualize yourself as that version of yourself. This Divine Higher Self, and live your day from Her perspective. You are one and the same. It's only the layers of daily crap that separate you, and sometimes we need someone else to remind us who we are under all that mess.

We also hope that you used the tarot/oracle spreads and found them useful. Go back to them when you may feel uncertain and need some additional guidance.

And most of all we hope that you will join us again for next year.

Pre-Order the 2021 Moon Journal!

Now that you've learned to call down the moon, set a sacred space, and create a ritual it's time to move beyond. Way beyond.

Visualize, imagine, or pretend...
You are standing outside under the light of the moon. There are a few wispy clouds, but She is shining brightly. The air is crisp but pleasant. The spring equinox is right around the corner.

You can smell the power in the air, it smells of ozone. Your hair blows in the gentle wind leaving you feeling so empowered.

You decide now is the time to get to work. You cast your circle. Perhaps you have a wand or just use the power of your forefinger. Either way, the power is within you and it is dying to come out. And unleash it you will.

You tuck away your wand and stand in the center of your circle. You lift one hand to the heavens and the other down towards Mother Earth, throw your head back to gaze upon the glorious moon and call her down to reside within you. The Divine Feminine is one with you.

Now.

Now is the time to work your magick.

Join us for next year's journal. It's going to get a little wild.

What you will find...
- All new rituals for 13 moons, including outdoor rituals
- Moon Cycle Crystal Guide
- Rituals for the Solstices
- Rituals for the Equinoxes
- All new tarot spreads
- And more!

Pre-order yours today!

About the Author

Kim began her spiritual path in 1991 at the Psychic Eye Bookstore where she walked out with a leather pouch of healing stones she would soon wear around her neck. Her path has twisted and turned and grown in so many different ways since then. Though that's when she first purposely started pursuing spiritual endeavors she had her first mediumship experience when she wasn't quite 2 1/2. Her mediumship and psychic abilities are something that has always been a part of her.

In 2009, she began her mindset and energy work and between the two realms-the mysticism of spiritual life and the powerful world of the mind-she's found a whole other universe exists from the one she once knew.

Kim is a Certified EFT Practitioner/Teacher, Certified Hypnotherapist, Certified Spiritual Life Coach, Reiki Master/Teacher, natural born Psychic Medium, a wild witchy woman, and a has had an ALMOST daily meditation practice since 2008.

hello@spirituallifepatheinstitute.com
www.spirituallifepathinstitute.com
www.facebook.com/spirituallifeseekers
www.instagram.com/spirituallifepathinstitute/
www.pinterest.com/spirituallifepathinstitutellc
www.twitter.com/slpillc
www.youtube.com/channel/UCreqjVLPlotKrrgxvTHDVzw

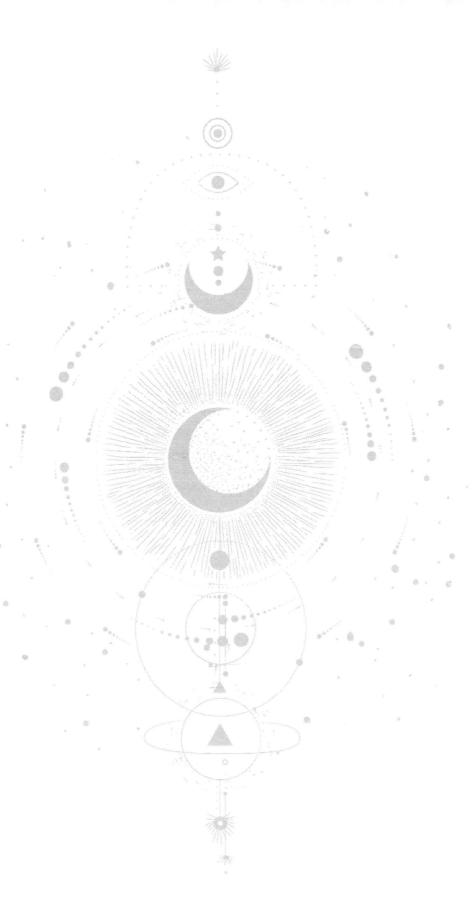

About the Designer

Anissa began her spiritual journey at the age of 13 when she attempted to commit suicide. When she survived, she quickly realized that there was a higher purpose for her life and decided to walk the path that has led her to where she is today. Growing up in a Puerto Rican household, she learned about Santería and the importance of honoring her ancestors. This is the basis of her spiritual practice.

She has experience as a self-taught graphic designer in addition to being a tarot reader and spiritual advisor. She currently owns The Oracle's Haven which is an online metaphysical boutique specializing in assisting all spiritual individuals on their path, regardless of whether they are just beginning or have been on their journey for a while.

She has a passion and a desire to help people see the best of themselves and has made it her mission to help people through the shadows.

hello@anissacosby.com
www.theoracleshaven.com
www.facebook.com/theoracleshaven
www.instagram.com/theoracleshaven
www.pinterest.com/theoracleshaven
www.youtube.com/channel/UCfvL_gBsb3taAEH53xnWOkQ

Made in the USA
Middletown, DE
08 January 2020